French Bulldog

Series "Fun Facts on Dogs for Kids"

Written by Michelle Hawkins

French Bulldog

Series "Fun Facts on Dogs for Kids"

By: Michelle Hawkins

Version 1.1 ~January 2021

Published by Michelle Hawkins at KDP

Copyright ©2021 by Michelle Hawkins. All rights reserved.

No part of this publication may be reproduced, distributed or transmitted in any form or by any means including photocopying, recording or other electronic or mechanical methods or by any information storage or retrieval system without the prior written permission of the publishers, except in the case of very brief quotations embodied in critical reviews and certain other noncommercial uses permitted by copyright law.

All rights reserved, including the right of reproduction in whole or in part in any form.

All information in this book has been carefully researched and checked for factual accuracy. However, the author and publisher make no warranty, express or implied, that the information contained herein is appropriate for every individual, situation, or purpose and assume no responsibility for errors or omissions.

The reader assumes the risk and full responsibility for all actions. The author will not be held responsible for any loss or damage, whether consequential, incidental, special or otherwise, that may result from the information presented in this book.

All images are free for use or purchased from stock photo sites or royalty-free for commercial use. I have relied on my own observations as well as many different sources for this book, and I have done my best to check facts and give credit where it is due. In the event that any material is used without proper permission, please contact me so that the oversight can be corrected.

French Bulldogs have a round head.

Another name for French Bulldogs is Frenchie.

French Bulldogs are very sensitive to other people's moods.

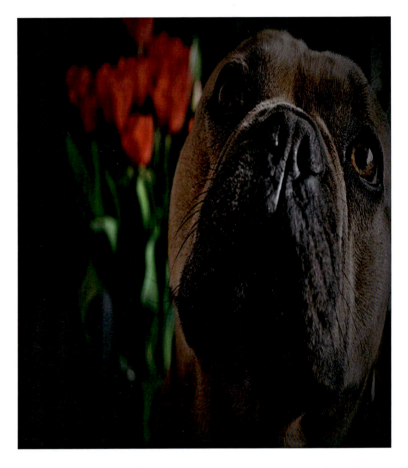

French Bulldogs were started in England.

French Bulldogs enjoy their owners encouraging them,

Bat ears are a sign of a French Bulldog.

French Bulldogs should weigh between sixteen to twenty-eight pounds.

French Bulldogs enjoy being cuddled.

French Bulldogs are very protective of their families.

A short fifteen-minute walk twice a day is adequate exercise.

French Bulldogs have either rose-shaped or bat ears.

French Bulldogs live to please their owners.

French Bulldogs are known to get along with other dog breeds well.

French Bulldogs need to be brushed at least once a week.

French Bulldogs are known to be a good companion.

French Bulldogs have a very muscular body.

French Bulldogs have a very squat like frame.

The facial folds on a French Bulldogs should be kept dry.

French Bulldogs make a good babysitter.

In hot weather, don't let French Bulldogs overexert themselves.

French Bulldogs are very affectionate dogs.

Never overfed a French Bulldogs due to them being prone to obesity.

French Bulldogs have very intelligent expressions on their face.

The average life span of French Bulldogs is ten to twelve years old.

Offer French Bulldogs treats occasionally.

Make sure that your French Bulldog gets bathed monthly.

French Bulldogs can be slow to be housebroken.

There was a French Bulldogs on the Titanic; only one of thirteen dogs on the Titanic.

Positive reinforcement is great if used with a French Bulldog.

French Bulldogs can be motivated by food.

If you scold a French Bulldog, they can be sad and mop around.

French Bulldogs enjoy being the center of attention.

French Bulldogs are a very adaptable dog.

French Bulldogs have a tendency to snort.

French Bulldogs enjoy making friends with humans.

French Bulldogs in France are called Bouledogue Francais, which means Ball Mastiff.

French Bulldogs are known to be easy to train.

French Bulldogs are always alert.

The average height of a French Bulldog is between eleven to thirteen inches.

Always make sure that French Bulldogs' nails are cut regularly.

French Bulldog's nose is much shorter than most dogs.

French Bulldogs is one of the top ten breeds in the United States.

Some airlines do not allow French Bulldogs to fly.

French Bulldogs can be a very stubborn dog.

French Bulldogs are patient with children.

French Bulldogs have no problem being in a crate.

French Bulldogs have a nickname called 'clown dog.'

French Bulldogs can not swim.

French Bulldogs should not be fed from the table due to the high-fat content of human food.

French Bulldogs can have health problems due to their short noses.

French Bulldogs are considered a very calm dog breed.

French Bulldog is a popular small dog for people who live in the city or apartment buildings.

French Bulldogs do not bark much at all.

French Bulldogs enjoy talking with their humans.

French Bulldogs are a cross between a toy bulldog and a ratter dog.

French Bulldogs have a very compact body.

French Bulldogs are omnivores; they eat meat and plants.

By brushing a French Bulldog, you will see new hair growth.

French Bulldogs do not need a lot of room to exercise in.

French Bulldogs are very playful.

Find me on Amazon at:

https://amzn.to/3oqoXoG

and on Facebooks at:

https://bit.ly/3ovFJ5V

Other Books by Michelle Hawkins

Series

Fun Facts on Birds for Kids.

Fun Fact on Fruits and Vegetables

Fun Facts on Small Animals

Fun Facts on Dogs for Kids.

Made in United States
North Haven, CT
18 March 2024